Up in smoke…

Alice Orhant

L'Aventurine

© L'Aventurine, Paris, 2000.
ISBN 2-914199-05-8

Table of contents

Tobacco: A gift from the New World   5
Tobacco graters   8
Snuffboxes   12
Pipes   26
Pipe tools   46
Pipe stands   50
Cigars   52
Cigar accessories   54
Cigar bands   60
Vistas   66
Lighting up   68
Cigarette holders   74
Smoking "oriental style"   76
Tobacco imagery   86
Bibliography   93

Tobacco: a gift from the New World

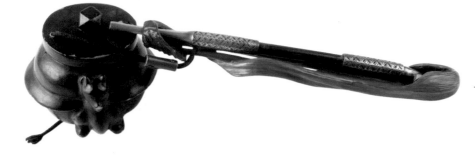

Pipe set. Wood and metal. Japan, 19th century.

Christopher Columbus was without doubt the first European to hold tobacco leaves in his hands, offered to him as a welcoming gesture. During his first voyage in 1492, his sailors met natives of the Taïnos tribe who smoked rolled leaves of a plant they called "cohiba". To all evidence, the smoking of them procured an enjoyable sensation. Without realizing it, the crew from Genoa had discovered tobacco and cigars. Tobacco first reached Europe via Spain brought back by caravels. In the 16th century, tobacco was used as an ornamental plant at the court of Lisbon. It first arrived in France in the port city of Rouen brought by boats arriving from Brazil. Normand sailors were the first in France to smoke pipes but the practice soon spread to Paris, the capital.

A royal endorsement

Around 1550, Jean Nicot French ambassador to Portugal during the reign of Marie de Medici discovered the medicinal properties of tobacco while in Lisbon. Used to treat colds, asthma and circulatory problems, it proved to be very helpful in alleviating the migraine headaches of the Queen Mother who was quick to promote its use. All members of the Court began taking snuff, and the indispensible accessory, the snuffbox, became the rage, often rivalling in luxury with the rich jewels of the courtiers. Although it was first sold by apothecaries under different names (Nicot's plant, the Queen's plant, "angoumosine", or "médicée"), it was later handled by grocers. It was then found in gaming houses and certain types of public houses with smoking rooms. In these places, pipes could be rented and tobacco was sold along with a glass of wine, beer or cider. The regular customers left their pipes on a wall-rack with their name or mark on them. They could smoke sitting or standing next to tables with brasiers filled with glowing embers.

Painted snuffbox. Gilt metal. France, 19th century.

5

Clay pipes were formed by hand then placed in copper molds. After a drying period of three or four days on racks they were fired in a kiln. The long, elegant lines of the stem were not due to esthetic rules but protected the smoker's mouth from the hot burning tobacco. The use of primitive materials and manufacturing techniques as well as the long delicate stem explain their extreme fragility and the high levels of production.

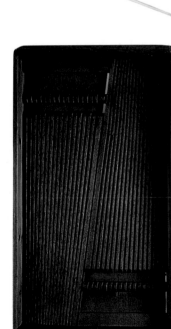

Tobacco for all

As tobacco passed from the salons of the Court to smoke-filled cabarets, it became available to an ever widening public. Snuff was reserved for delicate aristocratic and later bourgeois noses while chewing tobacco was for the unrefined tastes of the lower classes. It was as easy to tell a man's social class by his pipe and how he smoked it as it was by his clothes. The longer the pipe stem was, the more refined was its owner. The short stem clay pipe or nosewarmer identified the working classes. The French Revolution would change this smoking code. During the States General, chroniclers noted that nobles and the clergy took snuff while members of the Third Estate smoked pipes, having taken up this privilege formerly reserved for the upper classes. The Republic would in fact do its best to erase former class distinctions: the snuffbox was adopted as the official state gift and would become the rallying sign of the "Sans-culottes"; it was also adopted by the Army. But different shapes and materials utilized for the boxes would continue to identify social class distinctions.

For troop morale

The wars brought on by the French Revolution and the Empire provoked large migrations of peoples within Europe and the Near East. During the travels through England, the Germanic countries, Holland, and Russia, émigrés and soldiers discovered new types of pipes. There were also the novelty of narghiles in Egypt and Turkey, cigars in Spain and Portugal. Many soldiers had taken up smoking during the conflicts and continued when they returned home, passing on the habit to others. In Spain, cigars had been produced since the 18th century and in France, smoking was considered by the Romantic artists and writers as "the indispensible complement to the elegant and idle life" in the words of George Sand who knew what she was talking about! Anglomania was all the rage among the elite who proudly imitated the British dandies, among them Lord Byron who joined the other gentlemen in the smoking salon after dinner, so much so that the thick cigars smoked in the evening were nicknamed "after dinner" cigars. Equally imported from Spain, cigarettes were in the backpacks of many Napoleonic soldiers once the wars finished. They were home-rolled before being first manufactured in 1872. But the real fad of cigarettes started after World War I during the Roaring Twenties. Brand names reflect exotism, a yearning for distant shores, and leisure: Balto, Royale, Week-end, Gitanes, etc. With the advent of cigarettes and cigars, a complete line of accessories was developed for cigarette and cigar smokers as was the case for those who preferred pipes.

The Golden Age of pipes

The English aristocracy had adopted the pipe from 17th century while their French counterparts continued to prefer snuff for another two hundred years. The 19th century represented the Golden Age of clay pipes in France with many models decorated with designs and many others representing historical figures. To have one's face on a pipe was the irrefutable sign of a successful climb up the social ladder. To keep up with the demand, many pipe factories opened in France thus closing the production gap with their English, Dutch and German neighbors. Northern France already enjoyed an excellent reputation for the quality of its clay and welcomed new pipe factories which historians and collectors now consider as being among the most important of the times: Dunkerque, Charleville, Givet (the home of Gambier pipes). Delicate objets d'art, clay pipes could not compete with wooden pipes in durable wild cherry, pearwood, rosewood, or boxwood, prior to the discovery of briar by the craftsman of the French pipe center in Saint Claude. The perfect wood from a pipe smoker's point of view, it was also easily wrought. Discovered in Turkey in the 17th century, meerschaum would dominate production of luxury pipes throughout the 19th century and would inspire masterpieces created by the most talented craftsmen of the trade.

Tobacco roll. Belgium, late 19th century.

Plug or "carrot" cutter. Cast iron. Belgium, middle of the 19th century.

Until the end of the 18th century, tobacco was processed and sold in rolls for smokers and chewers. Leaves were rolled up and then twisted into long ropes (2 centimetres in diameter) which were then made into coils. These were sold in lengths. Carrots of tobacco were spindle-shaped and reserved for snuff. The distinctive shape would become the symbol of tobacconists in France.

Tobacco grater. Carved ivory. Dieppe, France, 18th century.
Right: *Tobacco grater. Carved wood and metal.* Flanders, 18th century.

Tobacco graters

Tobacco grater. Carved boxwood and metal. France, 18th century.

Tobacco graters first appeared in France during the 17th century. They were used until the middle of the 18th century when snuffboxes replaced them. At that period grated tobacco packaged by Royal workshops could be bought throughout France. Graters were luxury items destined exclusively for the aristocracy and the emerging bourgeoisie and hence a reflection of the social class of their owners. The most skilled craftsmen lent their talents in an effort to transform this quite commonplace utensil into true objets d'art. The finest woods were used - oak, beech, walnut, boxwood. Limoges contributed its expertise in enamel work. Shell, hardstones, horn and precious metals would also be widely used materials. Great care was taken in producing highly esthetic works of art. The designs, however, remained socially codified: coats of arms for the aristocracy, geometrical designs or biblical scenes for members of clergy, anecdotal (some show smokers using a grater) or bucolic scenes were appropriate for the lower classes. Mythological scenes were suitable for men of letters. True to nature, libertines were naturally drawn to erotic or pornographic scenes. Some models, however precious, are also functional and included storage containers. Some of the most amazing models from the Golden Age of graters are in iron with delicate inlay work while others are carved in ivory, a speciality of highly-talented craftsmen from the port city of Dieppe.

Tobacco grater, table model. Wood, ivory and metal. France, early18th century.

Pocket grater. Leather and iron. Western Europe, early 19th century.

Tobacco grater. Exotic wood and iron. Western Europe, late 19th century.

Tobacco grater. Ivory and iron. Western Europe, late 18th century. The powder collects in the shell.

Tobacco grater with snuffbox in the heel. Iron. Flanders, late 18th century.

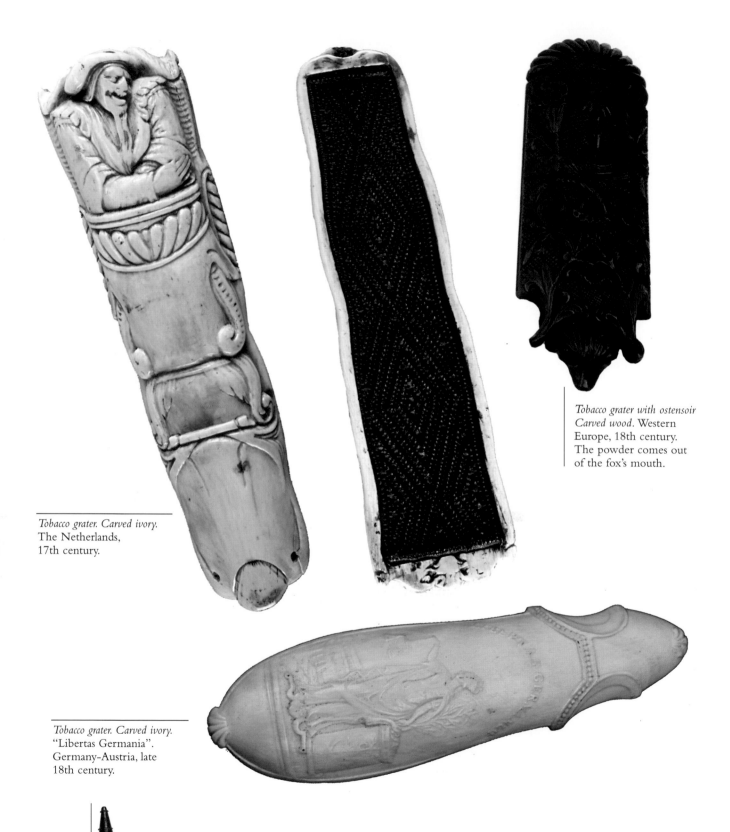

Tobacco grater. Carved ivory.
The Netherlands,
17th century.

Tobacco grater with ostensoir
Carved wood. Western
Europe, 18th century.
The powder comes out
of the fox's mouth.

Tobacco grater. Carved ivory.
"Libertas Germania".
Germany-Austria, late
18th century.

Tobacco grater with octopus. Carved ivory. France, 1680.

Tobacco grater with coat of arms. Carved wood. France, 1700.

Tobacco grater with double storage. Carved wood and metal. France, 18th century.

Snuffboxes

Snuffbox. Wood covered with plates of whale bone. France, 18th century.

Snuffboxes were first known in the Old World by the name "tabaquiere"; Molière coined the engaging expression "the small tobacconary storehouse" ("le petit grenier tabagique") for them. With the spreading availability of grated tabacco, owning a grater became unnecessary, and their vogue slowly declined. Snuffboxes became the new fad and the perfect gift for the rich and powerful to bestow on those they wished to honor or impress. The Comte d'Artois, the future Charles X, ordered no less than forty-seven snuffboxes as gifts to be distributed, during a visit to Spain. When the eight year old Mozart and his sister played before the court at Versailles on New Year's Day, 1764, how did Louis XV thank them? He presented them with snuffboxes in gold or shell with gold inlay, of course. These decorative objects survived fashion changes and social events which consequently modified materials, shapes, and styles. Snuffboxes undoubtedly reached their zenith during the reign of Louis XV. From a simple container, they evolved into quite sophisticated objects.

At certain periods of history, it is sometimes vital to be sure of the political opinions of those persons encountered in taverns or other public meeting

Snuffbox. Papier mâché. "Le matin à la brebis. Restez tranquilles." France, 19th century.

Snuffbox with combination. Copper. England, 18th century.

Snuffbox. Papier mâché. "Ne vous gênez pas", ("Help yourself!") France, 19th century.

Snuffbox. Painted bone. "Souvenir de N. D. de Lourdes". France, 19th century.

Snuffbox with historical scene. Carved wood. Germany, 19th century.

Oval snuffbox with floral motif in the Art Deco style. Silver and mother of pearl. France, 20th century.

Snuffbox with painted miniature of the Priest d'Ars. Bone. France, 20th century.

places. Snuffboxes proved to be one manner of demonstriationg political adherance. Boxes decorated with a picture of Voltaire, Rousseau or Diderot were very common in the years preceding the French Revolution. When the conflict turned France into a bloodbath, imagery of the taking of the Bastille prison or other contemporary historical "hotspots" became the fashion, expressing attachments to prevailing attitudes. Named after the family of Parisian henchmen, the Samson snuffbox, decorated with a picture of the guillotine, was also a much sought-after model; many grossly executed variations on this theme were produced. Snuffboxes and the imagery on outer and inner lids played a role in numerous conspiracies. Under the Consulat, the famous "Weeping Willow" snuffboxes were the rage among Royalists. A mourning woman was pictured in the shadows of a weeping willow near a funeral urn. The silhouettes of the late Royal family, Louis XVI, Marie-Antoinette and their son, the Crown Prince, were outlined on the sides of the urn and in the tree foliage. Numerous snuffboxes would later relate the political victories and setbacks of Napoleon Bonaparte who carried several with him to his final retreat on Saint Helena Island.

Snuffbox. Seashell. France, 19th century.

Left: *Snuffbox with squatting priest. Carved boxwood. France, 19th century. The powder is stored in the priest's back.*

Below: *Shoe-shaped snuffbox with secret opening mechanism. France, 19th century.*

Inner cover of snuffbox. Pressed burr. France, circa 1840. The scene evokes the return of Napoleon's ashes. "Il vivra toujours dans nos cœurs" ("He will always be alive in our hearts").

14

Snuffbox. Brown tortoiseshell inlaid with mother of pearl and silver filigree. France, late 19th century. Its curved form was designed to slip into the pocket of frock coats.

Above: *Snuffbox. Pressed birch bark.* Southern Germany, 19th century. The scene is probably from the La Fontaine fable "The Two Companions".

Right: *Engraved and painted snuffbox. Horn reinforced with brass.* France, 19th century.

Snuffbox with imperial eagle. Carved corozo nut, France, 19th century.

Snuffbox. Horn. France, mid-19th century. The Invalides in Paris are shown in the oval cartouche.

Snuffbox with Napoleon Bonaparte. Carved corozo nut. French Guyana, 19th century. The imperial eagle has the curved beak of a tropical bird. This is probably the work of a prisoner.

Round snuffbox. Papier mâché. France, 18th century.

The hidden inner cover of the snuffbox below showing Napoleon Bonaparte as a soldier.

Snuffbox with Napoleon as a Roman emperor. Carved wood. France, circa 1830. "J'ai gouverné sans peur. J'ai abdiqué sans crainte." ("I governed fearlessly. I abdicated unafraid".)

Snuffbox with Louis-Philippe. Carved wood. France, after 1830. "La Charité est désormais une vérité", ("Charity is henceforth truth".)

Snuffbox. Ivory and blue enamel with silver inlay. France, late 18th century.

Snuffbox with the attributes of music. Carved corozo nut. France, 19th century.

Publicity item for a brand of snuff. England, late 19th century.

SNUFF

J.W. HANCOCK

Rattail snuffbox. Carved wood with copper inlay. France, early 19th century.

Snuffbox. Engraved horn with brass hinge. France, 18th century.

Snuffbox. Carved burr. France, XIXe siècle. Napoleon is winking: "J'ai du bon tabac. Qui ne l'aime pas ne prenne le bac" ("I have good tobacco. Whoever does not like it, should not take the ferry")

Snuffbox with tarasque. Carved boxwood. France, 18th century.

Jokester snuffbox. Engraved horn. Germany, 18th century. Near the small opening (above) "I can only offer you my greetings" Near the large opening: "There will always be some for old friends".

Miser's snuffbox. Wood. France, 19th century.

Snuffbox with floral design. Carved bone. Work of an English sailor. 19th century.

Snuffbox with Napoleon Bonaparte. Enamel on gilt metal. France, 19th century.

Snuffbox with grape vine design. Carved boxwood. France, 19th century.

Snuffbox. Enamel with diamond inlay: "Mustapha, Prince of Princes". France, 19th century.

Snuff bottles. Internally painted glass. China, 19th century.

Snuff bottle. Internally painted glass. China, 19th century. The funnel and long spatula are in ivory.

Snuff bottles. Ivory and silver. China, 19th century. The small spoon is hand-shaped.

Snuff bottles called "secouettes". Stoneware. France, 19th century.

Snuff botttle. Chinese porcelain. China, 1960.

Snuff bottle. Coral. China, 1930.

Chinese snuff bottles

From 1650 on and for the next two and half centuries, snuff in China existed in powder form. The humid climate and the absence of flat pockets in clothing necessitated tight-closing bottles to carry tobacco. Another very specific problem, the extremely long fingernails of dignitaries, prevented them from taking a pinch of snuff between two fingers as was the tradition in the West. Small hand-sized phials or bottles were created with stoppers which contained a minuscule, built-in spoon in bone, ivory, or metal. Snuff bottles reflected the prestige and social status of the owner. Porcelaine, rock crystal, quartz, chalcedony, white or green jade, agate, or glass were favored materials during various dynasties.

Snuff bottle. Exotic nut and silver. China, 19th century.

Tobacco case. Carved coconut shell. Work of a prisoner on Devil's Island. Late 19th century.

Tobacco urn « The four pleasures » (Loving, Drinking, Dancing, Smoking). Bronze. France, 19th century.

Tobacco chest. Cast iron.
England, late
18th century.

Tobacco chest. Cast iron.
England, late
18th century.

Tobacco chest. Cast iron.
England, late
18th century.

Tobacco chest. Cast iron.
England, late
18th century.

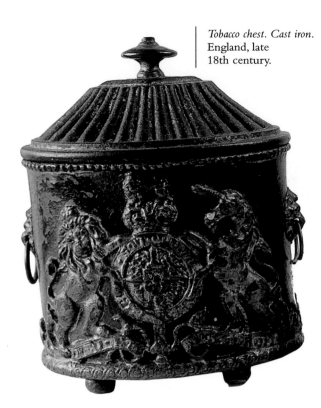

Tobacco chest. Cast iron.
England, late
18th century.

Tobacco chest. Cast iron.
England, late
18th century.

Tobacco chest. Cast iron.
England, late
18th century.

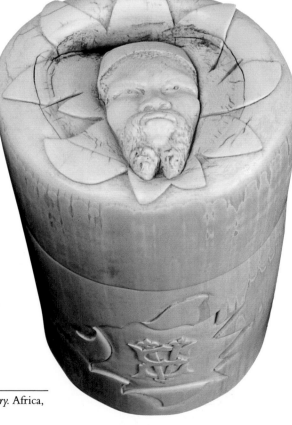

Tobacco pot. Ivory. Africa,
20th century.

Delft pots

First considered for its therapeutic virtues, tobacco was sold in the 16th century by apothecaries who stored it in terracotta and later in crockery pots as they did their other medicinal ingredients. When its sale was transferred to tobacco shops, the containers remained the same. Potters from the town of Delft in the Netherlands specialized in the manufacture of these items and largely dominated the European markets with pots of a highly characteristic shape. Although shapes evolved over the ages, they continued to be used throughout the 19th century. Inspired by models manufactured in Rouen, France, as well as porcelain containers from China, the ovoid shape would progessively dominate production. Although never outfitted with handles, their shape was such that they could easily be carried with little fear of breakage.

At its apogee, thirty different potteryworks were in production in Delft. Indissociable with the Dutch city, the signature blue color was probably inspired in part by the craze in Europe touched off by the porcelain imported from China. More prosaically, few colors could withstand the high temperatures necessary for the pewter-based glazing; cobalt blue was the most heat resistant. As time passed, buyers became accustomed to this color code reminiscent of the Colonial period and trade with China so potters remained faithful to this much loved Delft blue.

Delft blue tobacco pot. Earthenware and copper. The Netherlands, 18th century.

Tobacco pot. Porcelain and copper. France, 19th century.

Tobacco pot. Earthenware and copper. France, 19th century.

Pipes

Pipe. Painted terracotta. Belgium, early 20th century.

The oldest known image of a pipe is to be found in Palenque, Mexico on a bas-relief in a Mayan temple from the 6th century A.D. An officiant is holding a long pipe in his mouth from which thick smoke is pouring. The decorations on many Pre-Colombian clay and stone pipes indicate their use in magic or religious ceremonies. This perhaps exclusive use was not limited to South America because calumets were used for the same purpose in North America. In Sioux mythology, the different parts of the pipe were sacred representations of the universe. During his first voyage to the New World in 1492, Christopher Columbus described his surprise at seeing groups of natives walking around "with a small lit roll of a plant of which they inhale the perfume".

From the sacred to the common

In the Old World, it seems that the use of pipes and the name (from the Low Latin pipa: reed, pipe) only became significant from the beginning of the 17th century with the opening of several important pipes factories, notably in England. It was also in England that pipes would become widely popular, much promoted by Sir Walter Raleigh, Queen Elisabeth I's favorite, who in 1618 walked to the gallows, a pipe clenched between his teeth. With the generalization of the pipe in Europe, its tubular shape was modified to a curved or bent line. In 1617, the pipemaker William Baernelz, an English Catholic who had settled in Holland for religious reasons, opened the first clay pipe factory in the city of Gouda. They would soon be found all over Europe, as would models produced in Broseley and elsewhere in England from 1575 on. In the beginning, the simple models, imported from the New World were imitated. Between the 16th and the 19th centuries, the size of the bowl of clay pipes would increase, reflecting the widening availability of tobacco and lower prices.

The first sculpted pipes appeared in the 18th century. In France, Dunkerque, Saint Malo and Marseille were great pipe-making centers; in the 19th century, such illustrious houses as Fiolet and Gambier participated in the grand art of clay pipes. Over the centuries, pipes were also produced in wood, much more resistant than clay. But it was not long before smokers realized that certain woods like wild cherry or oak denatured the taste of tobacco. It was not before the middle of the 19th century that the ideal wood was discovered: briar from heather roots. Meerschaum would prove to be the first natural material to give complete satisfaction, but its price and fragility reserved it for the wealthy who appreciated its originality and refinement.

Pipe. Painted terracotta, bamboo and metal. Manufactured by "A.K." Belgium, 19th century.

Pipe. Terracotta.
Manufactured by Gambier.
France, 1880.

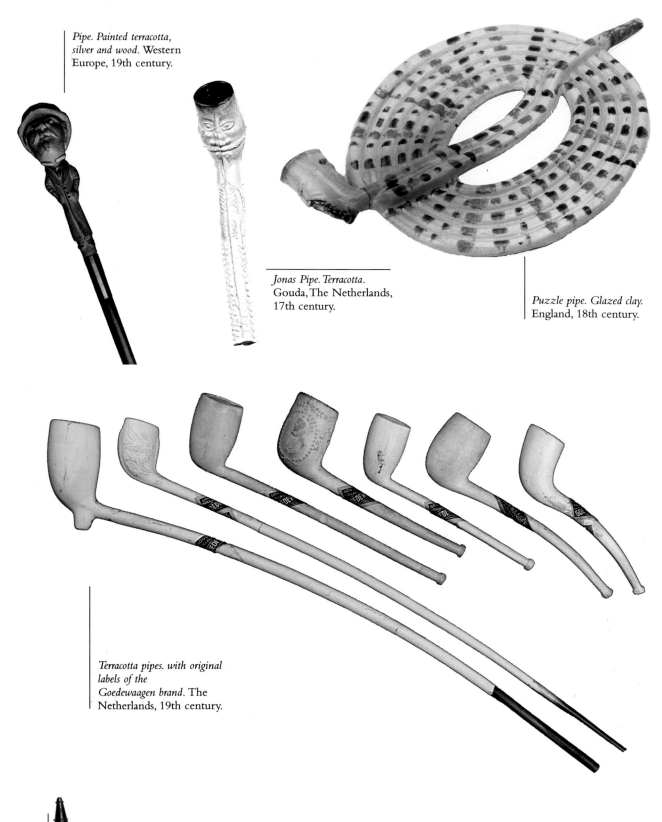

Pipe. Painted terracotta, silver and wood. Western Europe, 19th century.

Jonas Pipe. Terracotta. Gouda, The Netherlands, 17th century.

Puzzle pipe. Glazed clay. England, 18th century.

Terracotta pipes. with original labels of the Goedewaagen brand. The Netherlands, 19th century.

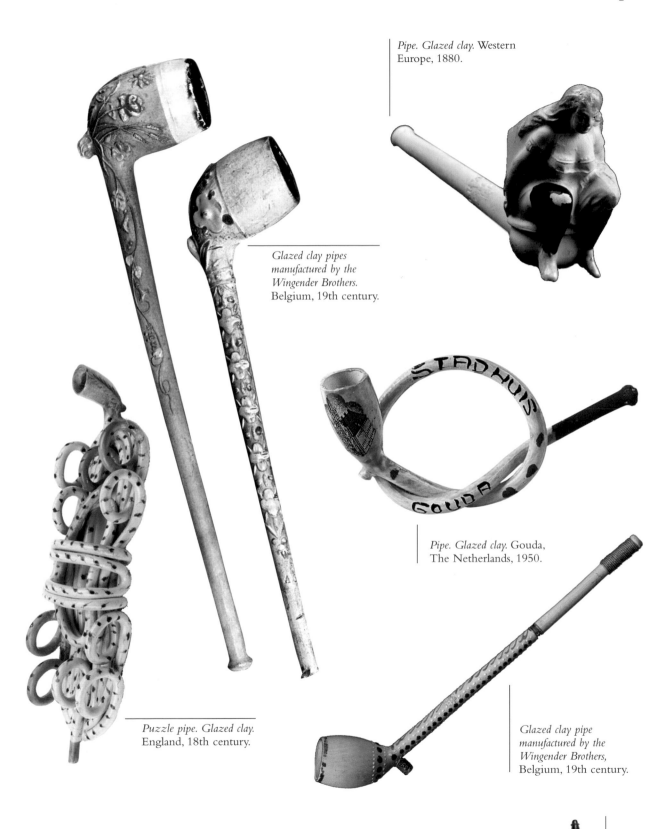

Pipe. Glazed clay. Western Europe, 1880.

Glazed clay pipes manufactured by the Wingender Brothers. Belgium, 19th century.

Pipe. Glazed clay. Gouda, The Netherlands, 1950.

Puzzle pipe. Glazed clay. England, 18th century.

Glazed clay pipe manufactured by the Wingender Brothers, Belgium, 19th century.

29

Pipe. Meerschaum and silver. Austro–Hungarian Empire, early 19th century.

Ulm pipe. Wood and silver. Germany, 19th century.

Ulm pipe. Wood and silver. Germany, early 19th century.

Pipe. Meerschaum and silver. Austro–Hungarian Empire, early 19th century.

Ulm pipe. Wood and silver. Germany, early 19th century.

Ulm pipes

From the 16th century until the discovery of briar root, several varieties of wood were utilized for pipemaking in Europe. Only the densest hardwoods (oak, beech, and notably wild cherry) and those whose combustion levels are slower than that of tobacco were longlasting. Perhaps since wood altered the taste of tobacco, these pipes enjoyed limited popularity with the exception of those produced in and around the German town of Ulm. From the middle of the 17th century, their originality assured their fame, throughout Europe. Shaped from a piece of alder or boxwood selected for the beauty of the grain, the bowl was frequently ornamented by silver embellishments. Ulm pipes were often decorated with a silver mantle attached to the stem by a silver chain. The mantle served as a cover which slowed combustion and offered protection from wind and rain. It also prevented flying sparks from causing fires. In fact, most of the workers in factories and workshops were pipesmokers.

Pipe. Meerschaum and silver. Austro–Hungarian Empire, early 19th century.

Ulm pipe. Wood, ivory and silver. Germany, early 19th century.

*Pipe with love scene.
Meerschaum and silver
with amber mouthpiece.
Western Europe, early
19th century.*

*Imperial pipe.
Meerschaun and silver
with wooden mouthpiece.
Western Europe, early
19th century.*

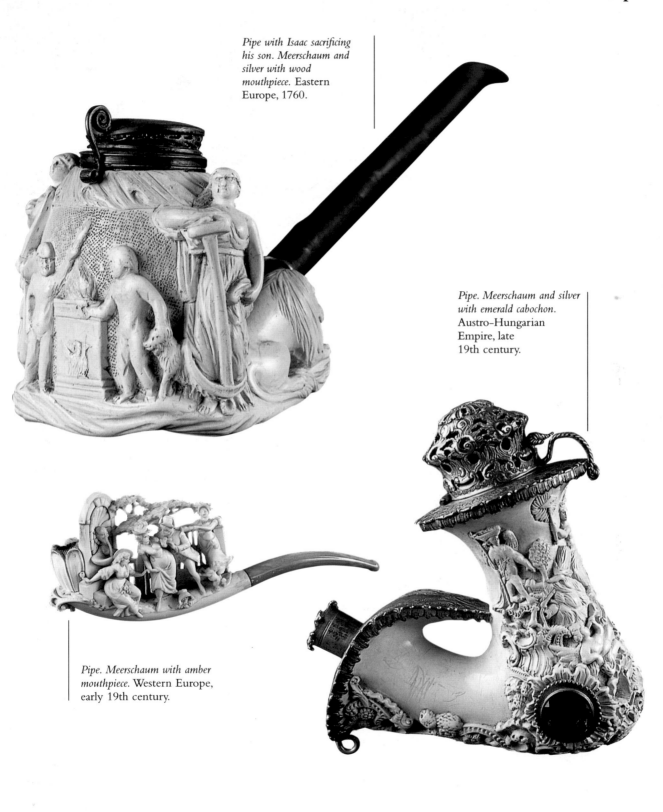

Pipe with Isaac sacrificing his son. Meerschaum and silver with wood mouthpiece. Eastern Europe, 1760.

Pipe. Meerschaum and silver with emerald cabochon. Austro-Hungarian Empire, late 19th century.

Pipe. Meerschaum with amber mouthpiece. Western Europe, early 19th century.

Pipe. Meerschaum with amber mouthpiece. Austro-Hungarian Empire, early 19th century.

Meerschaum pipes

Meerschaum – which literally means "seafoam" in German – actually has nothing to do with the sea. The white mineral is composed of magnesia, silica and water and is still today extracted from mines in Anatolia, Turkey. Easily wrought, meerschaum has permitted the creation many of the most precious masterpieces of the art of pipes. Many are set with silver mantles and amber mouthpieces, and are true miniature sculptures using the same classical themes: busts and human figures, animals, mythological, hunting or love scenes. Meerschaum pipes were very expensive and were obviously reserved for the aristocracy and rich merchants.

The first meerschaum pipes were probably produced in Turkey where the mineral was first discovered. Their popularity first grew in Hungary during the first half of the 18th century before spreading to the rest of the continent. Since then, meerschaum pipes have been coveted objets d'art of the rich and influential.

Pipe. Meerschaum with amber mouthpiece. England, 19th century.

Pipe. Meerschaum with amber mouthpiece. England, 19th century.

Case with three pipes representing Bayern princes. Meerschaum with amber mouthpiece. Germany, early 19th century.

Pipes. Meerschaum with amber mouthpiece. Austro-Hungarian Empire, early 19th century.

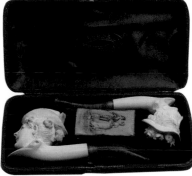

Faces on pipes

In the 19th century – the Golden Age of clay pipes – sculpted pipes with human faces were the fashion. The Gambier pipe factory in France was one of the best known manufacturers of them. Arthur Rimbaud immortalized these extremely popular pipes in the first stanza of *Oraison du soir* (1871) "… a Gambier/Clinched in his teeth, with air billowing intangible sails". The speciality of this factory which produced more than 100,000 pipes per day from 2,000 different models were celebrity pipes of real (Victor Hugo, Napoléon Bonaparte, Léon Gambetta) or fictive (La Paimpolaise, Gervaise) characters. Each enjoyed its moment of glory while never being able to rival with the Jacob pipes which represented an aged bearded man wearing a turban. Although the origin of the name remains unprecise, the incredible success of this model can be attributed to the long flowing carved beard which remains cool when the pipe is lit.

Case with two pipes. Meerschaum with amber mouthpiece and porcelain match case. Western Europe, early 19th century.

Pipe. Meerschaum with amber mouthpiece. Austro-Hungarian Empire, early 19th century.

Jacob pipe. Meerschaum with amber mouthpiece. Western Europe, 19th century.

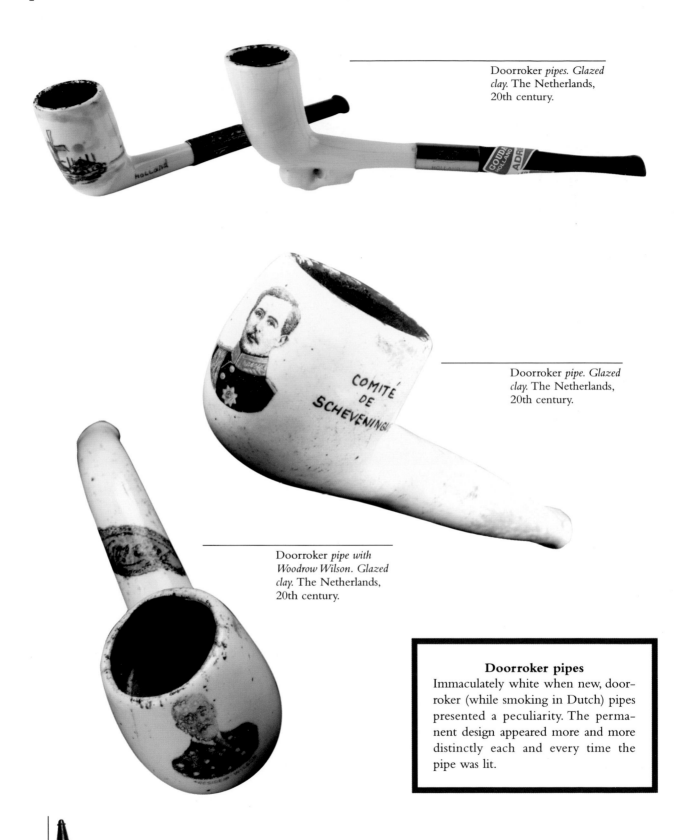

Doorroker *pipes. Glazed clay.* The Netherlands, 20th century.

Doorroker *pipe. Glazed clay.* The Netherlands, 20th century.

Doorroker *pipe with Woodrow Wilson. Glazed clay.* The Netherlands, 20th century.

Doorroker pipes
Immaculately white when new, doorroker (while smoking in Dutch) pipes presented a peculiarity. The permanent design appeared more and more distinctly each and every time the pipe was lit.

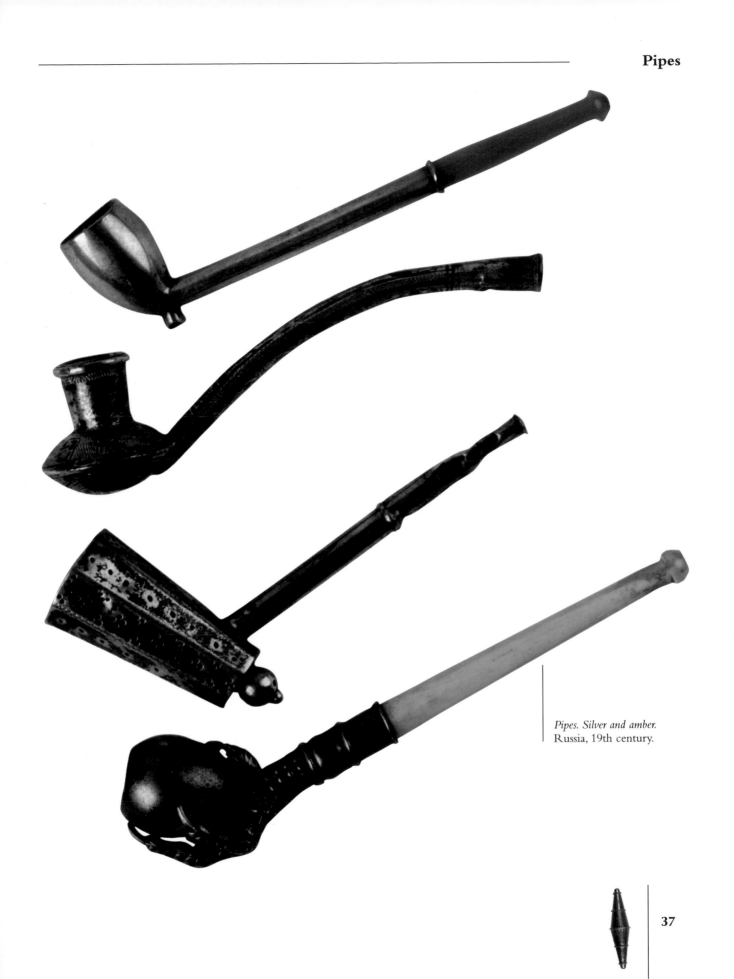

Pipes. Silver and amber.
Russia, 19th century.

Porcelain pipes

Resistant although easily wrought, porcelain pipes, first appearing in 1710 in Germany, surpassed all others. The Meissen manufactory was renowned for its models of decorated pipes. In the beginning of the 19th century, numerous craftsmen, "Hausmalers", started painting porcelain pipes to customers' wishes. In France, the Sèvres Manufactory proposed various models of pipes in its catalogue a number of which representing Napoleon Bonaparte. The reservist's pipe or "regiment pipe" was first produced in Germany in the late 19th century and then spread to France and Austria. During the reign of Wilhelm II (1888-1918), the conscription was reinstated and the military profession was overrated. Commemorative objects (porcelain pipes, beer steins, cups) became all the rage among reservists who had their name and those of their fellow soldiers, the name of the garrison town and corresponding dates painted on these objects. Military parades, battle scenes or soldiers in uniform were favorite themes for the decoration of pipe bowls. Most of these pipes remain anonymous works since very few artists signed their work. The bowls were covered with a mantle usually in the shape of the regiment's helmet ("pickelhaube" for infantry soldiers and "ulhans'tschapka" for the cavalry). Stems could measure from 35 to 200 centimeters long and were composed of several parts, the most important being the ring or cube in staghorn. When text and drawings painted on the bowls also appear on the stem, it is a guarantee for collectors. Although reservists' pipes were produced by the thousands, there are few complete pieces now existing due to the fragility of porcelain and the fact that only the porcelain bowls were considered of real interest.

Pipe. Horn, porcelain and wood. Germany, XIXᵉ siècle.

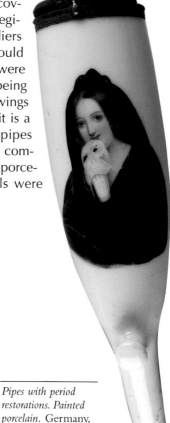

Pipes with period restorations. Painted porcelain. Germany, 1820–1830.

38

Pipes. Painted porcelain. Germany, 1820–1830.

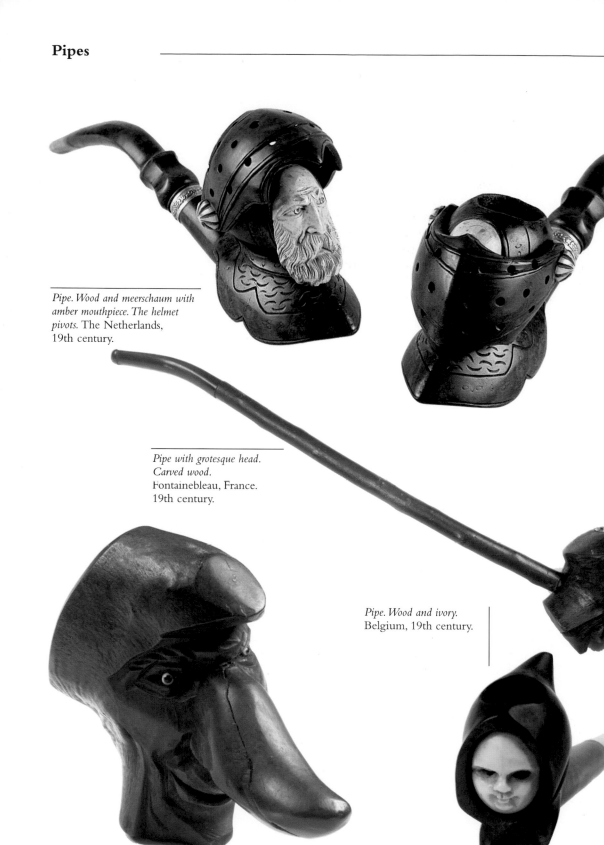

Pipe. Wood and meerschaum with amber mouthpiece. The helmet pivots. The Netherlands, 19th century.

Pipe with grotesque head. Carved wood. Fontainebleau, France. 19th century.

Pipe. Wood and ivory. Belgium, 19th century.

Wooden pipes

Oak, alder, elm, walnut, wild cherry, boxwood, burr: many different woods using different hewing techniques were tried by craftsmen and smokers in search of appropriate pipe materials. It is a pity that the person who first discovered briarwood which is in fact heather root remains anonymous to this day for he certainly deserved to have a pipe carved in his image. In any case, the discovery was heaven sent for Saint-Claude, small village in the Jura mountains, as briar pipe production there developed rapidly from the 1850's on. Since that time, it has been considered the perfect pipe material: esthetic, lightweight, durable, and resistant to the high temperatures of hot tobacco.

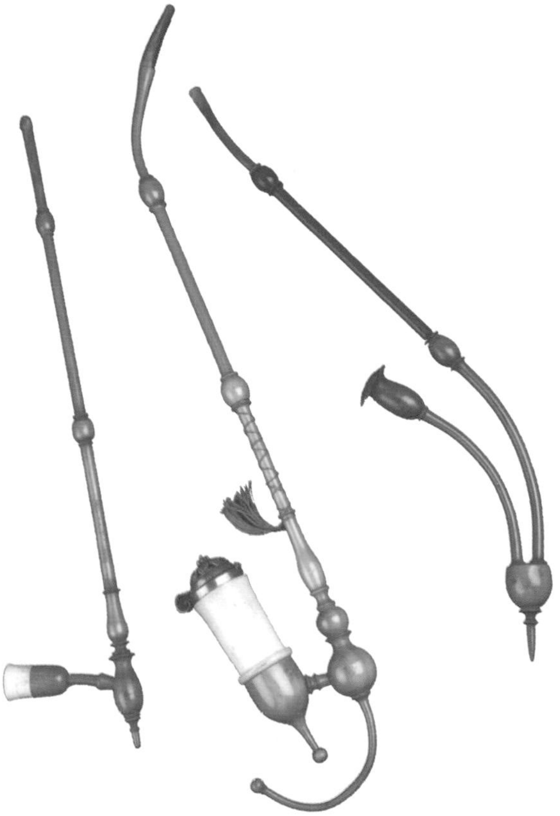

Three pipes. Turned wood and meerschaum.
Saint-Claude, France, 19th century.

Pipe with harvest scene.
Carved boxwood and silver.
Germany, 1740.

41

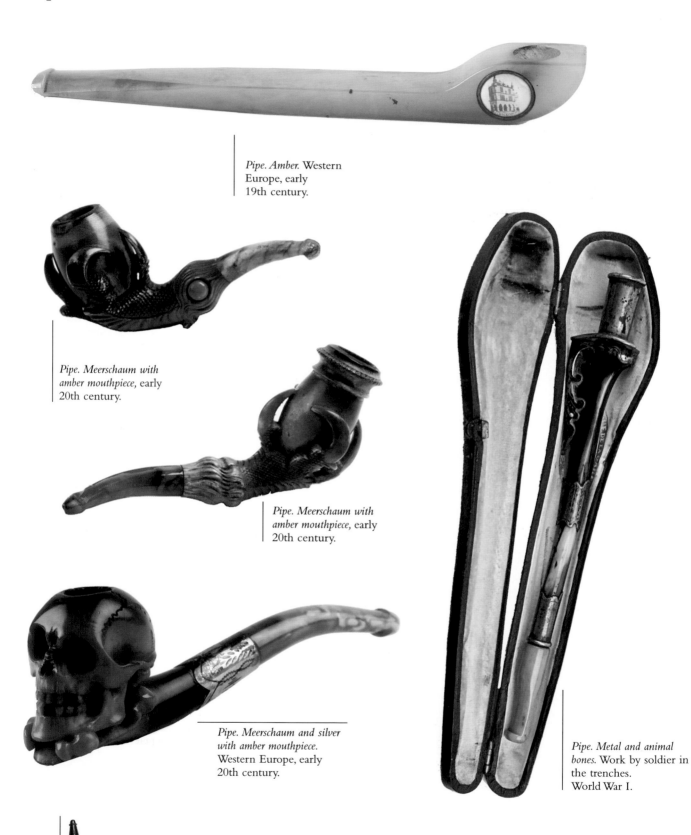

Pipe. *Amber.* Western
Europe, early
19th century.

Pipe. *Meerschaum with
amber mouthpiece,* early
20th century.

Pipe. *Meerschaum with
amber mouthpiece,* early
20th century.

Pipe. *Meerschaum and silver
with amber mouthpiece.*
Western Europe, early
20th century.

Pipe. *Metal and animal
bones.* Work by soldier in
the trenches.
World War I.

Cigar holder with owl on a branch. Meerschaum with amber mouthpiece. Western Europe, early 20th century.

Pipe with owl on a branch. Meerschaum. Western Europe, early 20th century.

Pipe. Meerschaum with bamboo stem. Germany, late 19th century.

Pipe. Meerschaum with amber mouthpiece. Western Europe, 19th century.

Pipe. Meerschaum with amber mouthpiece. Western Europe, early 20th century.

Pipe. Wood with amber mouthpiece. Belgium, early 20th century. The puppies are visible when the mother dog rocks back.

Pipe. Animal paunch covered in terracotta. The Cameroons, circa 1900.

African pipes

It was in the middle of the 19th century that pipes from Africa began appearing in the Western world. But it was not until the 1930's and the impassioned interest of Alfred Dunhill in them that these "idols of pagans" became all the rage among European collectors. In a multitude of shapes and fashioned from a wide variety of materials – terracotta, wood, ivory and metals – African pipes, even the most common ones, always carry the mark of a creative spirit and often have symbolic meaning. In the Cameroons, the puffy cheeks of the faces sculpted on brass pipes recall the trumpet-playing heralds who preceeded the kings of the Banum tribe on their journeys.

Pipe. Terracotta. The Cameroons, circa 1900.

Pipe. Wood. Congo, early 20th century.

Pipe. Ivory. Central Africa, early 20th century.

Following page:
Ceremonial pipe, called playing pipe. Copper and bronze. Benin, early 20th century.

Pipe tools

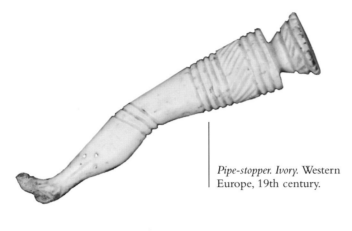

Pipe-stopper. Ivory. Western Europe, 19th century.

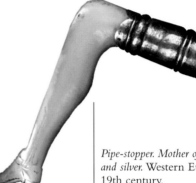

Pipe-stopper. Mother of pearl and silver. Western Europe, 19th century.

Pipe-stopper with Mr. Pickwick, Charles Dickens' character. Copper. England, 19th century.

Smokers, meticulous as they are, attach great importance to keeping clean pipes. If a pipe is not properly maintained, it can become foul as it becomes saturated with tars which seriously alter the tobacco taste. Willow twigs, blades of grass, straw and reeds were among the early solutions to this problem. As smoking became more sophisticated, pipe tools followed this trend and many models were fashioned from bone, ivory, silver and gold. While domestics used their thumb to press down the tobacco, lords and masters tended to use pipe-stoppers of all shapes. Many models are in horn with a flattened silver head decorated with animal or political themes. In more libertine circles, pipe-stoppers were often in the shape of a woman's leg which unveiled on a miniature scale what propriety of the times demanded be hidden.

Pipe-stoppers with historical characters. Copper. Western Europe, 19th century.

Top, from left to right: William IV of Germany, Wellington, George III of England.

Bottom, from left to right: Galileo, René Descartes, William Shakespeare.

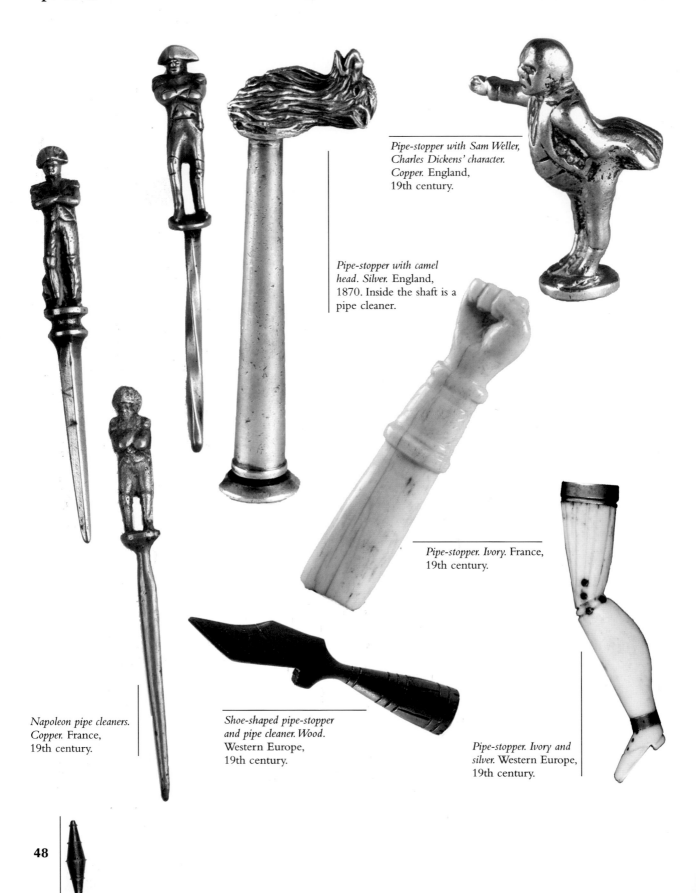

Pipe-stopper with Sam Weller, Charles Dickens' character. Copper. England, 19th century.

Pipe-stopper with camel head. Silver. England, 1870. Inside the shaft is a pipe cleaner.

Pipe-stopper. Ivory. France, 19th century.

Napoleon pipe cleaners. Copper. France, 19th century.

Shoe-shaped pipe-stopper and pipe cleaner. Wood. Western Europe, 19th century.

Pipe-stopper. Ivory and silver. Western Europe, 19th century.

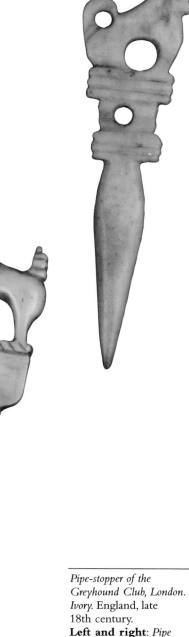

Pipe-stopper of the Greyhound Club, London. Ivory. England, late 18th century.
Left and right: *Pipe cleaners with animals. Ivory. Western Europe, 19th century.*

Pipe stands

From the 16th century, public places of relaxation sprung up following population shifts. Certain places brought together those who wanted to enjoy a smoke. Later it also became a popular activity in taverns and public houses where a glass of cider or beer accompanied pipe smoking. Regular customers took their clay pipe wallrack, identified by a number or by a distinctive mark, from a wallrack. The pipes hung vertically to counter the effects of condensation. Clay pipes were very fragile and in homes were placed in decorative pipe stands to store and protect them. Pipe rests also became common domestic objects and were produced in wood and stone. They became standard items of English, Delft or regional porcelain factories.

Pipe stand. Turned wood and metal. The Netherlands, circa 1850.

Pipe stand. Turned wood and metal. The Netherlands, circa 1850.

Pipe rest. Porcelain. England, 19th century.

Pipe rest. Porcelain. France, 19th century.

Pipe rest. Wedgewood porcelain. England, 19th century.

Pipe. Terracotta. The Netherlands, late 18th century.

Trompe l'œil *pipe stand. Painted wood.* Western Europe, early 20th century.

Cigars

Box of Prior cigars.
Belgium, 1905. The bands represent the first 25 American presidents from George Washington to Theodore Roosevelt.

Although cigars were known in Europe since the first voyages of Columbus, more than three centuries were needed to establish the term cigar itself. They were called for a long time "rolls" or "sticks of tobacco". In their birthplace, Cuba, they were and still are called "tabacos". It is now thought that the word "cigar" probably originated from the language of the ancient Mayans and the word "Ciq-Sigan". It would not be accepted by all because in 1700, Father Labat preferred "cigales" then "ceegar" in the English dictionary published in 1735 before being transformed into "cigare", "cigarro" among others. This lexical hesitation would continue well into the 19th century: the Encyclopedic Dictionary by Brockhaus in 1833 listed still other forms: "cigale", "segares", and "cigaren". If the first "modern" cigars appeared in Seville in 1626 and in France more than a century later, the first known brand name, "Bernardino Rencurel", was registered in Havana in 1626. The same year "Cabanas y Carbajol" was also created. As they constituted a defense against counterfeiters and fakes, brand names caught on quickly in Cuba and became synonymous with quality. When the state monopoly of Madrid was lifted, a multitude of private factories began production and soon were competing for smokers' favor: "Partagas" (1827), "Por Larranaga" (1834), "H. Uppmann" (1844), "El Rey del Mundo" (1848), "Romeo y Julieta" (1850). Others included: "Arturo Fuentes", "Bolivar", "Cifuentes", "Hoyo de Monterrey", "Maria Guerrero", "Rafael Gonzales", "Sancho Panza".
The brand names are now part of the history of cigars, although the actual names of the factory owners changed several times. Factory and cigar brands were often family affairs and as such were subject to the risks and hazards of inheritances. Several factories were acquired in that way in the late 19th century by American companies. Others closed ("La Imperiosa", "Senora Cubana", "Antilla Cubana").

Bunch of cigars wrapped in coconut husks. Philippine Islands, early 20th century.

Presentation box of La Corona *Cuban cigars used by salesmen.* Circa 1900.

Box of Wilhelm II cigars with French customs stamp. 1906.

Cigar-cutter. Copper.
Western Europe, 1870.

Cigar-cutter. Copper and
ivory. Western Europe,
1870.

Cigar accessories

Cigar-cutter. Brass. France,
19th century.

Cigar-cutter. 18 carat gold
and metal. Western
Europe, 1870.

In the early 19th century, French, Spanish and Italian cigars made with tobaccos imported from various places of origin were shipped in packages which varied according to their size and number and changed from brand to brand. During the middle of the century during the Golden Age of cigars and the advent of the major brands, Havana cigars were shipped in uniform boxes of lightweight, durable Cuban cedar. These boxes keep their shape and pleasant color over very long periods of time. To this day, Havana cigar boxes are still made from this odorless and porous material which allows the cigars, a "live" product to breathe. The standard box contains 25 cigars in two layers of 13 and 12 pieces separated by a cedar sheet. For the same quantity or for 50 or even sometimes 100 cigars, there are squarish cabinets. Sometimes they are presented in bundles or bunches held together by a yellow ribbon. The inner and outer sides of the lid are emblazoned with the brand name, and medals won in international competitions are proudly displayed.

If the tip of the cigar can easily be opened with a fingernail or bitten off as is the custom in Cuba, in less humid climates like our own, a specific tool is used so as not to damage the tip. The cigar cutter can either be a small, well-sharpened penknife, small scissors with curved, softly bevelled blades or a "guillotine" in table or pocket models. Other systems used screw augers or still others made V-shaped notches in the tips. Lancets which plunged an inch or more into the filler were also in fashion at certain periods.

A cigar case is without a doubt the most useful accessory for preserving cigars. Today some have humidifiers which correct low humidity levels, preventing the wrapper from drying out, splintering or breaking off.

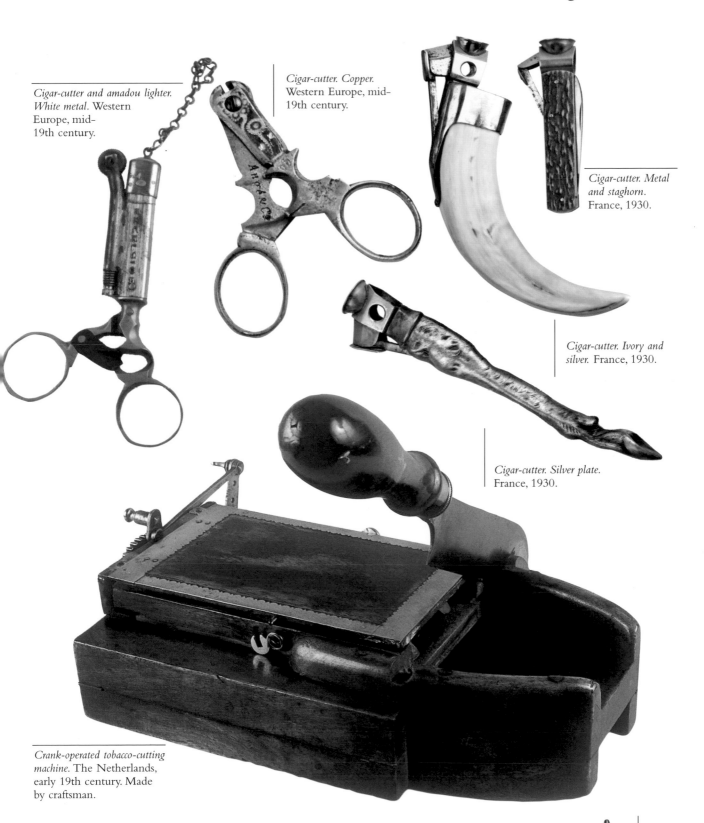

Cigar-cutter and amadou lighter. White metal. Western Europe, mid–19th century.

Cigar-cutter. Copper. Western Europe, mid–19th century.

Cigar-cutter. Metal and staghorn. France, 1930.

Cigar-cutter. Ivory and silver. France, 1930.

Cigar-cutter. Silver plate. France, 1930.

Crank-operated tobacco-cutting machine. The Netherlands, early 19th century. Made by craftsman.

Three-hole cigar-cutter. Silver and metal. France, 1920.

Bunch of Pannecoucke cigars. Belgium, prior to 1905.

Left and below: *Cigar-cutters. Copper.* Western Europe, 1870.

Bunch of Pannecoucke cigars. Belgium, prior to 1905.

Publicity cigar-punch for Augé et Hatton champagne. France, early 20th century.

Four cigar-cutters in ivory, copper and silver. Publicity items for various brands of champagne. France, circa 1904.

Cigar-cutter. Copper and metal. Western Europe, 1930.

Cigar-cutter and punch. Copper and ivory. Western Europe, 1880.

Cigar-cutter and punch. White metal. Western Europe, 1880.

Cigar-holder. Meerschaum with amber mouthpiece. Western Europe, 19th century.

Cigar-holder. Meerschaum with amber mouthpiece. Western Europe, 19th century.

Cigar-holder. Meerschaum with amber mouthpiece. Western Europe, 19th century.

Cigar-holder. Carved staghorn with amber mouthpiece. Western Europe, 19th century.

Cigar-holder. Meerschaum with amber mouthpiece. Western Europe, 19th century.

Cigar-holder. Meerschaum with amber mouthpiece. Western Europe, 19th century.

*Egg-shaped cigar chest.
Mother of pearl and copper.
France, 19th century.*

Cigar chest. Silver. Western
Europe, 19th century. The
cigars are stored vertically.

*Cigar chest. Wood and silver
plate. France,
19th century.*

*Musical cigar chest. Onyx
and silver.* Japan, 1920.

Cigar rest. White metal.
France, 19th century.

59

Band for bunch of cigars.
Philippine Islands, early
20th century.

Band for bunch of cigars.
Early 20th century.

Cigar bands

Following page: *Cigar bands of heads of state.* Early 20th century.
Left from top to bottom: Wilhelm I, Edward VII, Bismarck, Von Moltke, George Washington, Queen Wilhemina.
Right from top to bottom: Wilhelm I, Léopold II of Belgium, Czar Nicolas II, King Victor Emmanuel of Italy.

Bands are the rings of often brightly colored paper which embellish and personalize cigars. Legend has it that they were first used by English dandies in the 18th century. Zino Davidoff in his book The History of Havana Cigars evoked the role of those Beau Brummels who rolled a paper band around the head of the cigar to protect their delicate fingers or gloves from tobacco or nicotine stains. However, the attested father of this custom inherent to all good cigars is Gustave Block, a Dutch dealer who in 1850 had the idea of banding the Havana cigars he sold for publicity purposes. This elementary marketing tactic was quickly adopted by cigar manufacturers who wanted their products to be distinctive. On October 25, 1884, the Havana Cigar Manufacturer's Union officially adopted the band and opened competition among union members for the most colorful, richest, most interesting designs. In this extremely competitive race, red and gold dominate the palette of colors. Today still, the hand-made cigars are also banded by hand before they are boxed. These paper rings are held together by plant-based glue and placed at the same level of each cigar thus enhancing the visual harmony of the filled box. Collectors all over the world search and exchange these small bands of paper. Among the most prized are those of discontinued brands from the 19th century.

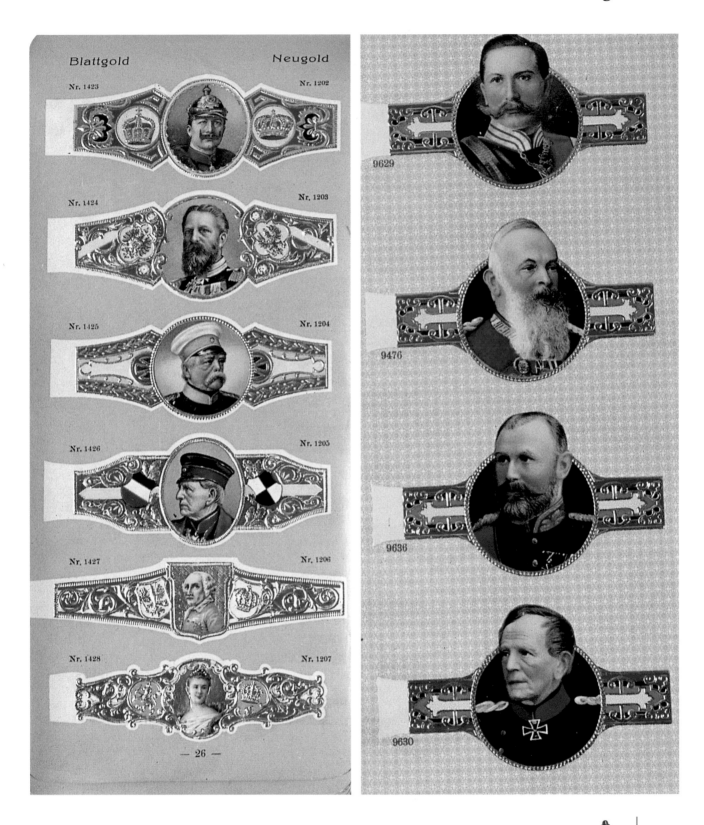

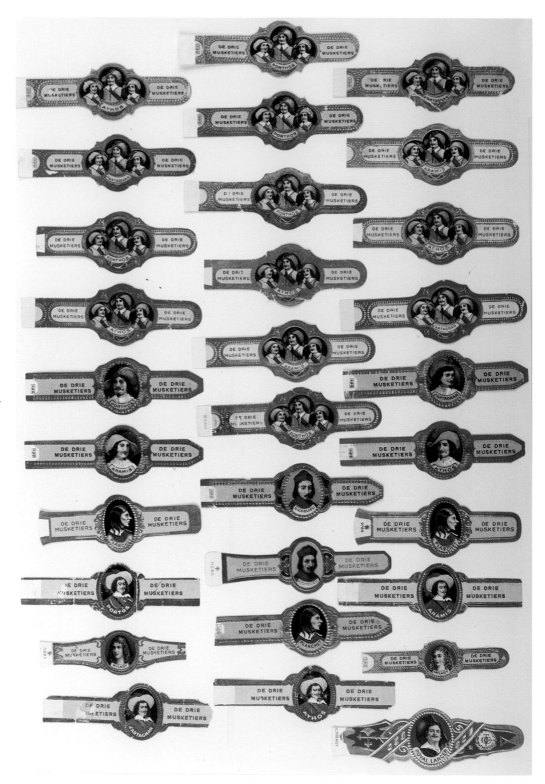

Series of The Three
Musketeers *cigar bands.*
The Netherlands, circa
1920.

Cigar bands of various Cuban, Mexican, Belgian and American brands. Early 20th century.

Cigar bands of various historical figures. Early 20th century.
Left from top to bottom: Bismarck, Edward VII, Jefferson Davis, Prince Henrik, Napoleon.
Right from top to bottom: Bismarck, Edward VII, Edward VII, Abraham Lincoln, Wilhelm II, Leopold II of Belgium.

Bands of cigars especially made for various heads of state. Early 20th century.

Vistas

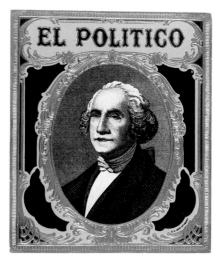

Upon opening a new box of cigars, two things strike the eye: the well-organized presentation of the cigars and the sumptuous vista provided by the large decorative image printed in chromolithography decorating the inside cover of the lid. A wide range of subjects in the most luxuriant colors were utilized: mythology, history, allegories, bucolic imagery. But women, very accessible women, were by far the preferred subject of inspiration, by those who designed the images as well as by those who bought the cigars. Today still the picturesque fantasies are a source of joy for collectors.

In 1912, in an attempt to limit counterfeiting, first Cuba, followed later by other cigar-producing countries, began placing a seal on cigar boxes as a guarantee of origin. For Havanas, the seal was green; on the left of the oval cartouche were placed the arms of the Republic and on the right, a plantation scene with three palm trees. "Republica de Cuba" was printed in large letters in four languages, German, Spanish, English and French, followed by "Guaranteed by the Cuban government to be cigars exported from Havana". While less spectacular than the vistas, these seals are still prized collectors' items.

Above and following page: *Inner and outer cigar box labels for various brands representing Presidents George Washington and Abraham Lincoln.* 20th century.

Lighting up

Domesticating the flame is an ongoing problem; already in the 17th century smokers lighted their pipes using ember tongs. This is clearly shown in different period paintings. Another method used at the same period involved rounded copper containers filled with embers and hung near a fire. Small pieces of wood placed nearby were easily ignited when brought in contact with them. Later the strips of wood were replaced by small rolls of paper. This system would be used for centuries and ember tongs remained in service until the First World War.

Produced in all shapes and materials, "pyrogènes" with their rough striking surface for lighting matches became common objects on café tables: brasiers were found on the tables of public houses throughout Europe. Certain pyrogènes doubled as pipe rests or cigar lancets. A popular model during the reign of Louis-Philippe represented an Oriental man wearing a turban. World War I would bring about the demise of pyrogènes. In post-war times, they were no longer set out on café tables as waiters always carried matches or a lighter in their pocket. In use since the 14th century, amadou, a fongic material, was easily ignited by a spark caused by steel struck against a flintstone. In fact, the principle used for the firing mechanism of a pistol would also be utilized to invent the cigarette lighter. The domestication of the flame moved into modern times in the 19th century when experimentation with phosphorus by German and French chemists led to the invention of matches.

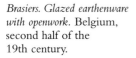

Brasiers. Glazed earthenware with openwork. Belgium, second half of the 19th century.

Counter pipe lighter on city gas. Turned wood and copper. The Netherlands, early 20th century.

Counter lighter. White metal. France, early 20th century.

Counter lighter. White metal. France, early 20th century.

Counter lighter. "Le premier essai" ("The first try") White metal. France, early 20th century.

Counter lighter. "Un anglais à Paris" ("An Englishman in Paris") White metal. France, early 20th century.

Brasier. Copper with wooden handles. The Netherlands, 19th century.

Tripod brasier with spatula. Copper with wooden handle. The Netherlands, 19th century.

Counter lighter. Copper. Germany, circa 1880. This model was also carried by street cigar vendors.

Brasier in the Antique style. Silver. Western Europe, 19th century.

Counter lighter on city gas. Metal. The Netherlands, circa 1920.

Brasier. Silver. The Netherlands, early 20th century.

Match box and pocket pyrogène. *Chrome brass.* France, late 19th century.

Match box and pocket pyrogène. *Brass and deerskin.* France, late 19th century.

Counter pipe lighter on city gas with cigar-cutter. The Netherlands, early 20th century.

Match box and pocket pyrogène. *Brass.* France, late 19th century.

Ember tongs with pipe-cleaner. Iron and glass beads. France, 19th century.

71

Match box. Brass. France, 19th century.

Lighter showing a German general smiling in Paris and crying in Verdun. Brass. Work by soldier in the trenches. France, World War I.

Match holder and wall pyrogène. Juniper. France, late 19th century.

Amadou friction lighter. Silver and vermeil. Switzerland, 1898. Shooting award.

Pipe warmer. Brass with wooden handle. France, early 19th century.

Ember scoop. Wrought iron. France, 18th century.

Amadou friction lighter. Silver plate. France, late 19th century.

Case of friction lighter. Copper. France, 19th century.

Match box and pocket pyrogène. *Chrome brass. France, late 19th century.*

Pyrogène. *Turned boxwood. France. 19th century.*

Cigarette-holders

Cigarette-holder. Enamel with amber mouthpiece. France, circa 1930. A spring mechanism ejects the cigarette butt.

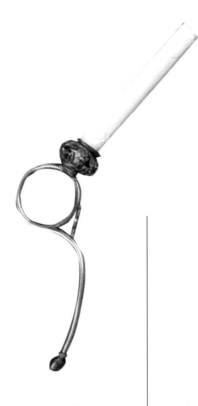

It was only in 1953 that the first filter-tip cigarettes were commercialized. Prior to that, cigarettes, which had started their successful world campaign after the Revolution of 1830, were rolled more or less tightly in another plant, often a corn leaf. But if in France Jean Bardou manufactured cigarette papers from 1838, wisps of tobacco stuck out the ends and bothered elegant dandies and certain elegants ladies won over to the passion of tobacco. In smoking salons, it was considered chic to smoke cigarettes placed in an elegant holder in ivory, blown glass, amber, shell and meerschaum. Their refinement was equal to those of pipes sculpted from the same materials.

Cigarette-holder ring. Silver. England, circa 1900.

Matching set of cigar and cigarette-holders. Red amber. Germany, circa 1900.

Cigarette-holders. Europe, early 20th century. **From left to right:** *bone, fish-shaped; silver with red amber mouthpiece; ivory; painted ivory; silver with yellow amber mouthpiece, ivory and wood; silver with red amber mouthpiece.*

Smoking "oriental style"

Evocative of distant lands and exotic dreams, the Near East and tobacco have always been good partners. Very early on, different cigarette manufacturers utilized oriental imagery. Between 1900 and 1915 in order to compete with American and English cigarette brands, French companies established in Algeria used local beauties to adorn their packs and advertisements. This seduction campaign was aimed at legionaries to win them over to the charms of such brands as Bastos, Melia, Alba, la Semeuse, and Le Nil among others. The practice of "drinking smoke" first appeared in the Arab countries about four centuries ago. The basic model from which water pipes were developed was very simple. From this evolved the narghile (from the Persian word "nargile", in reference to the bowl containing water). In numerous Islamic cities, smoking in groups through flexible tubes was considered the height of conviviality. When the smoke reached the lips, it had been cooled by the perfumed water in the pipe. The materials, shapes and sizes vary widely in these pipes, from simple clay to precious Bohemian crystal.

Water pipe. Silver, copper, turned wood and terracotta. Southern Asia, 19th century. The water supply is in the base.

Below and previous page: *Cigarette tins. Chromolithograph on metal. Early 20th century.*

Water pipe. Copper. Surinam, 19th century. The water supply is stored in the bird.

Water pipe. Earthenware, terracotta, metal and wood. Southern Asia, 19th century.

Cigarette tins on Oriental themes. Chromolithograph on metal. Early 20th century.

79

Cigarette tins on Egyptian themes. Chromolithograph on metal. Early 20th century.

Previous page:
Advertisement for "ALBA" cigarettes. Algeria, circa 1900.

Cigarette tins on Oriental themes. Chromolithograph on metal. Early 20th century.

Cigarette tins on Oriental
themes. Chromolithograph
on metal. Early
20th century.

Following page:
*Advertisement for
"ALBA" cigarettes.*

84

Tobacco imagery

Cigarette tin. Chromolithograph on metal. Germany, early 20th century.

Tin of pipe tobacco. Chromolithograph on metal. United States, early 20th century.

Tin of pipe tobacco. Chromolithograph on metal. United States, early 20th century.

Cigar tin. Chromolithograph on metal. Europe, early 20th century.

Cigarettes were first launched in France in 1843. They were first sold in cylindrical packets of twenty, with little care given to packaging. It was only in 1880 that the cardboard packages of the cigarettes produced in state-owned factories in France began to be replaced by metal tins which were far more practical for carrying pipe tobacco or cigarettes while preserving aroma. These boxes or tins were ideal for advertising which obviously would evolve with changing trends. From 1880 to 1930 Egyptian and Turkish-inspired imagery would dominate literally hundreds of French, German, English and American brands. A perfect example of the fascination with oriental subjects, Old Joe the camel has been the symbol of Camel cigarettes since 1913. Smokers' fantasies were also attracted by Europe and the Roaring Twenties before turning to the United States and more particularly to Hollywood and its captivating stars of the silver screen.

Tins of pipe tobacco. Chromolithograph on metal. Europe, early 20th century.

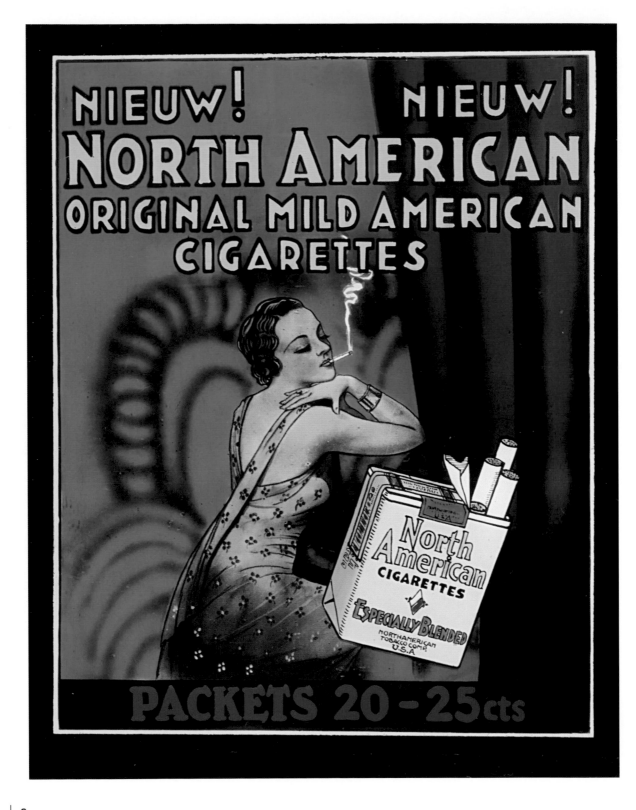

Previous Page: *Slide projected during intermission in cinemas. Belgium, circa 1930.*

Cigarette tins. Chromolithograph on metal. France and England, early 20th century.

Above and following page: *Advertisements for the Veuve Pannecoucke & Fils Tobacco Company.* Courtrai, Belgium, prior to 1905.

Fabrique de Cigares Fins
Cigarettes - Tabacs en feuilles et coupées
Vve **Pannecoucke & Fils**

Bibliography

Bastien (A.P.). *La Pipe,* Paris, 1973.
Deschodt (E.). *L'ABCdaire du cigare,* Paris, 1996.
Dunhill (A.). *The Pipe Book,* Londres, 1969.
Lecluse (J.). *Pipes d'Afrique Noire,* Paris, 1985.
Liebaert (A.) et Maya (A.). *La Grande histoire de la pipe,* Paris, 1993.
Maya (A.). *L'ABCdaire de la pipe,* Paris, 1996.
Nourrisson (D.). *Histoire sociale du tabac,* Paris, 2000.
Tillie (J.). *Le Tabac de Dunkerque,* Dunkerque, 1992.
Vigié (M. et M.). *L'Herbe à Nicot,* Paris, 1989.

Collective works:
Casparek (G.), Hill (S.), Hufnagel (W.), Pollner (O.). *La Passion de la pipe,* n.l., 1984.
Encyclopédie du fumeur, Paris, 1975.
Le Livre de la pipe et du tabac, Académie internationale de la pipe, 1998.
Le Livre de la pipe, Académie internationale de la pipe, 1997, 1998, 1999.

Catalogues:
Tabac et Sociétés, Catalogue, Tobacco Museum, Bergerac, France, 1991.
Catalogue, Seita Tobacco Museum, Paris, 1992.

The vast majority of the objects presented belongs to the exceptional collection Walter Vanden Bulcke. Without his knowledge, generosity and kindness, this book would never have been possible

We would also like to thank all the following persons who participated in this project: Marc Feldman, Dominique Delalande, Madame Leblic, as well as Hélène Breton, Le Louvre des Antiquaires and Madame Ann Matton, curator of Tabak Museum.

Louvre des Antiquaires
2, place du Palais-Royal
75001 Paris

Dominique Delalande
1, allée Majorelle
Téléphone: 33-1-42-60-19-35

Galerie des Arts — Ouaiss Antiquités
15-17 et 18-20 allée Riesener
Téléphone: 33-1-42-61-56-99

L'Herminette
6, allée Germain
Téléphone: 33-1-42-61-57-81

Au Passe Partout
21, rue Saint-Paul
75004 Paris
Téléphone: 33-1-42-72-94-94

Tabak Museum
Marktstraat 100
8530 Harelbeke
Belgique
Téléphone: 32 56 733 470

Sources of illustrations:

Walter Vanden Bulcke Collection — pages 6, 7, 8 right and bottom, 10, 11, 14, 15, 18, 19 left, 20-33, 35, 38, 39 top, 40-43, 45, 46 left and bottom-right, 47 left and right, 48-51,52 top and bottom, 53-68, 69 right, 71 center, 72-73, 74 bottom, 75-89.
Dominique Delalande Collection — pages 9, 19 right, 36-37, 47 center, 39 bottom, 44 right, 45 bottom left, 46 center and right, 74 right.
Marc Feldman Collection — pages 12, 13, 14 top left, 15 top right, 16, 17 left, 38 center, 52 center, 69 left and center, 70, 71 top and bottom.
L'Herminette Collection — pages 8 left, 44 right.
Collection Ouaiss antiquités — page 17 right.
Collection Tabak Museum — page 34.

Photographies: © Robert Canault.

Photoengraving: Édilog, Paris.
Translation: William Wheeler

Printed in Italy by Grafedit
August 2000